In A World That Worships Illusion

In A World That Worships Illusion
A Treasury of Love

Carolyn Jean

iUniverse, Inc.
New York Lincoln Shanghai

In A World That Worships Illusion
A Treasury of Love

Copyright © 2008 by Carolyn Jean

All rights reserved. No part of this book may be used or reproduced by any means, graphic, electronic, or mechanical, including photocopying, recording, taping or by any information storage retrieval system without the written permission of the publisher except in the case of brief quotations embodied in critical articles and reviews.

iUniverse books may be ordered through booksellers or by contacting:

iUniverse
2021 Pine Lake Road, Suite 100
Lincoln, NE 68512
www.iuniverse.com
1-800-Authors (1-800-288-4677)

Because of the dynamic nature of the Internet, any Web addresses or links contained in this book may have changed since publication and may no longer be valid.

The views expressed in this work are solely those of the author and do not necessarily reflect the views of the publisher, and the publisher hereby disclaims any responsibility for them.

ISBN: 978-0-595-47719-7 (pbk)
ISBN: 978-0-595-91981-9 (ebk)

Printed in the United States of America

Contents

You 2

LOVE CREATES LOVE~

A is A 6
An Offering 7
Loving Another 9
A Wench 10
The Feeling of You 12

AND LOVE CREATES PAIN~

Pain 17
Hangover 20
A Walk in the Park 25
Intervening Spaces 26
Anger 29
Love is a Flower 30
Speculation 31

AND LOVE CREATES MORE LOVE~

Risk 35
Old Lovers & Friends 36
The Reunion 40
You Said, "I've always loved you" And Then There Was Music! . . . 42

Pocket Love 44
Higher Than High 45
Joy 50

SOMETIMES, LOVE JUST CREATES~
Little Boys & Big Dogs 57
The Lure of the Dunes 58
My Friend 60

ANOTHER LOVE~
A Masterpiece 65

ACKNOWLEDGEMENT AND DEDICATION 69

In a world
that worships illusion
and gazes on a liar's moon,
depicting what was
as what might have been
and what is
as what would have been "nice"
and what can be
as what cannot be,
you are the reality
to which I can cling.

Within your mind
is a sanctity of space
affording me quiet peace
and emotional balm
for the horrors
of this life
as it is,
immortalization
of all that is joyous,
and celebration
for the aliveness
of our mutual soul.

You

you are the best,
the best
part of me
you are the part
that smells
the sunshine,
and feels
the sound
of wind in the trees,
and tastes
the warm, sweet smell
of flowers,
and touches
the sight
of high, high mountains,
and sees
the feel of my body
next to yours.
you satisfy
all my senses,
my Love,
all my senses you satisfy.

Love Creates Love~

one hundred million
years ago
there was only space—
then it was
touched with life
and showered with Love

A is A

what do
any of us have
that is
any more valuable,
any more permanent,
any more fleeting,
any more painful,
than
Love?

for those
who love,
Love becomes at once
all things

An Offering

if you will accept my love, I will
   promise you nothing except

      Friendship~
          as long before I loved you,
          I liked you

      Devotion~
          unblinded, but subject to
          no external determination

      Understanding~
          inexhaustible as our verbal
          and physical communications

      Warmth~
          as steady as the emotions
          you kindle in me

              . . . .

Sympathy~
    as deep as the need your
    mind and body express

Pride~
    in you as a man
    and equally as a human being

Respect~
    of your accomplishments,
    your failures… and your privacy

Possession~
    of all that I am, or may be,
    because of you

Freedom~
    to reject this offer,
    even after its acceptance

Loving Another

Loving another is first
    loving one's self

The loved self
    gives freely
    receives willingly
    has space to expand and explore
    knows peace as freedom
        and a source of creation
    has depth
    and perception

The loved self
    accepts Love
    in a pure, raw
    naked form
    knowing
    that one day
    it may
    spread restless wings
    and fly away

A Wench

Love,
so soft, so gentle,
grasps you by the hand,
teaches you to walk-
to walk a new path.
surrounds you in a blanket
of delicate, sweet warmth.
makes you know why
greek gods spilled their wrath.

Love,
with tenderness,
quietly rapes your mind-
your heart—your soul.
bends the strongest oak
like a graceful willow.
a Lovely fickle wench,
demanding to be needed—
leave her alone—one moment—
she slips from your pillow.

my Love
is a mirror
of my
experience of you

The Feeling of You

I wonder,
as I wake at night
and feel the warm security
of my body next to yours,
how it is possible
to love you—anyone! to such a depth
I am your possession.

I marvel,
as you stir gently
and my body moves with yours
that it is possible
that I have no needs, no wants
when I am with you.

I am content,
completely, as I absorb your warmth
and breathe deeply
of the special, delicious scent of you.
I am happy-
I desire nothing more.

acknowledge
my Love
and you acknowledge
your own
creation

And Love Creates Pain~

Pain

does pain
find its own way
to our door
or do we
seek it out
with sweet invitation?

does it
slash our wrists
without passion
or do we
put out our hands
begging to bleed?

why should pain
single out some
and not others?
is it perhaps
because some
embrace it lovingly?

. . . .

and in what disguise
does it woo us?
> the fragile white of the virgin ...
> the bronzed gold of a lover ...
> the bitter green of jealousy ...
> the indigo of faith and loyalty?

pain strikes
in the pit
of the stomach,
washes violently
over the
heart and soul,
And imbeds itself
like a cancer
in the mind

. . . .

it serves
its own purpose
and we try to hide—
> in the false gaiety of alcohol ...
> in the oblivion of drugs ...
> in the absorption of work ...
> in the violence of the animal ...
> by slamming the doors of our minds ...

its damage
created,
pain finally departs,
leaving in its
place
deep and ugly scars

the scars
shrink and fade,
only as the mind dictates.
if the source
can be accepted,
the soul lives.

Hangover

after the joy
of sharing
your bed,
nights alone hold
no surprises,
no celebration,
no desire,
no peaceful feelings

. . . .

I drift
in and out
of restless sleep,
or from
room to room,
seeking refuge
from my mind
and my body

. . . .

escape,
I cannot,
from memories
of your skin,
your fragrance,
your touch,
the climaxes
of our Love

. . . .

warily
I sigh,
and drink coffee
and watch
blackness
turn to gray
turn to another
Damn day

. . . .

if my heart
turned to stone
and my mind
to blessed
blankness
my body
could forget
you never

A Walk in the Park

without you, my darling,
    the days are lonely and barren—

like the park trees whose
    leaves long ago fell to the ground;
children climb in and out
    of bright plastic free forms,
making a game of the maze—
    practicing, perhaps, the game of life?

as bits and scraps of paper
    swirl 'round in the winter breeze,
so do thoughts of you
    swirl constantly through my mind
how could I have known
    you'd touch more than my hand?

the sun drops behind the hill
    and tears on my face grow cold.
it would have been less painful
    had you not stopped by my life.

        I wouldn't have
      missed it for the world

Intervening Spaces

my body
misses your body
(how could it not!)
and I miss
the pleasure of you
lighting my cigarette
(and being able to light yours),
making my coffee
(tastes better than mine),
playing the music I like,
making certain
the bed is warm
before we crawl in,
allowing me to rub your back—
but most of all,
oh, God!—
how I miss
the intimate sharing
of our minds

. . . .

that which I hold
most precious
in this life,
that which I have
been able to share
with only two others —
both female,
one a daughter,
neither as I share with you —
that which
can make me crazy
and return sanity as well.
that which
expresses my Self,
and sometimes
confuses my Self,
that which remains
solely mine
no matter what else
the world may strip
in its passing fancy

. . . .

that which I give
to you
because
you earned the right
to take it,
that which enables me
to give to you—
my body—
not just allow you
to use it—
it is that ultimate sharing
which I miss
the most
when our physical spaces
are intervening spaces

Anger

anger
is a healing process
of its own.
anger
is green, black and blue
in color.
someone
once said it was red—
but
that's bullshit…
everything is bullshit—
life is bullshit—
love is bullshit—
perhaps
anger is bullshit, too

Love is a Flower

running,
    down hill ...
        a lovely flower,
           beautiful,
                undoubtedly fragrant
                    flower.

never
    took time to
        stop
            running.
                fragrance?
                      undoubtedly pleasing
                        fragrance?
              falling,
            down the hill!!
            crying,
        wondering,
            did it have
                fragrance?
                    shall I ever know?

                    wilting
                    dying~~~

Speculation

morning comes, I wake
loving you
at night I go to sleep
loving you
all this love
so much love
what shall I do with it
if you don't want it?

give it to another?
an amusing thought at best
always you would be there
between, yes.
around, under
I tried it before
I go no place without you
addicts are always addicts

. . . .

learn not to love—
less painful, I wonder?
"learned nonexistence"
programmed
protection—
impossible
like learning not to breathe
or a daisy growing thorns

accept life as it is?
square one once again
and after acceptance?
change, not life, changes

all this love,
    so much love
what shall I do with it
if you don't want it?

And Love Creates
More Love~

Risk

ferret out
with
dispassionate analysis
the illusion of safety

that weakness
which strives
to deceive your mind
of the
impermanence of Life

and leaves behind
only
bittersweet reflections
tinged
with pain
and resignation

Life's only risk
is in
taking no risk

Old Lovers & Friends

there is
a comfortableness,
an incredible freedom
if you will,
known only by
old lovers and friends
(I remember
you like
your coffee black)

in the shelter
of our past,
in the Love
we once tried to share
there is
no need
to act or perform
(you always left
tooth paste
in the sink)

. . . .

no need
to prove how marvelous
we are—
both in and out
of bed
we are
what we are—
that's marvelous!
(I always had to do
the damn dishes
first)

you didn't fit
my picture,
the one I created
you to be,
and likewise I failed
to fit yours
so we tore up
the pictures—
and our love

. . . .

we each
wanted to be
right,
traded being right
for being
happy
and ran to seek
our separate ways
other sinks —
more dishes
and tooth paste

we can
go for it,
my Love,
everything or nothing
both the same
choose
to have it all
or give it up
you are
what no one else
can ever be

. . . .

you may
return to your
other love
and I may
return happily
to mine
comfortable
in the space
we share
known only by
old lovers and friends

The Reunion

on a soft summer day
    in the sun,
scent of pine trees
    filling the air,
we dusted off
    the pages of long ago,
recalling when
    we were the perfect pair.

we were young, beautiful,
    much too busy,
and didn't take the time
    to share our love.
I had only wanted then
    to be your girl,
which was as natural
    as the clouds above.

you heard the words,
    but not what I said,
kept putting work
    and worry in my place
so I took our children,
    ran far away,
traded being happy
    for saving face.

. . . .

other loves we both
    tried to substitute,
as years went by
    on our separate roads.
joy and happiness
    were only fleeting things
recreating us
    made frustrating loads.

by some miracle
    we sit here in the sun,
touching and sharing
    our hurt and love.
so many special ways
    we said "I love you,"
even more natural
    than those clouds above.

a lizard ran across
    the dusty road
and you wiped
    the tears from my face.
I am your other self
    and you are mine,
truly a relationship
    we cannot replace.

You Said,
"I've always loved you"
And Then There Was Music!

it filled the air
drifting among the pines
crescendoing over the mountains
staccotoing on wild flowers

a distant golden harp
carried the poignant melody
of a love so nearly forsaken
and a life lost, sought and found

cymbals and a timpani
on statuesque rock
and my ears crashed like thunder
with knowledge that you cared

. . . .

lovely strings and a guitar
laced through wind blown grass
and wrapped around my heart
making it bleed for pain I had caused

a lonely wailing horn
completed the mighty orchestration
as I searched deeply in your eyes
and knew the conductor to be you

there was music everywhere
joyous, vibrant and alive —
it lifted my soul in harmony
and awareness
of the celebration of life

Pocket Love

slip your hand in your pocket,
    that's it—down in the corner—
if your day needs fixin'
    or the world feels cold—
if you just want to share
    a smile, a tear, a daisy or so—
if you have no reason at all
    slip your hand in your pocket—
tucked down in the corner
    You'll find me always there.

hidden among your pocket change,
    the house key and a gum wrapper—
that's the place I've been
    damned near from the start—
even when at first I was afraid
    yours I absolutely chose to be—
love is letting go of fear and
    loving you, Baby, is all there is—
so slip your hand in your pocket
    you'll find me always there.

Higher Than High

I love
your body—
all of it

your
physical warmth
radiates
through me
and makes me
glow
from the inside

your arms
are strong—
but gentle—
they enfold me
with
a security
like a baby
must feel
at a mother's
breast

. . . .

your lips
first tender
with caresses
make me
tremble—
then
feel hunger—
as they explore
and demand
more

my fingers
trace
your back,
your nipples,
your navel—
everywhere
they find pleasure

. . . .

all
of your hair
is exciting
from that
of your
moustache,
which tickles
my face,
my neck,
my belly,
my thighs,
to that of your armpit
where I
bury
my face

. . . .

your
special smell
is intoxicating
before—
and after
our love making—
when evidence
of our satisfaction
lingers
throughout the night
and I
taste me
in your morning
kiss

and when
you are in me
I rejoice—
your gentleness
and roughness
arouse passions
I did not know
exist
and I want you
to stay
there
forever

. . . .

as we
fall asleep
and as your movements
arouse me
during that sleep
I know
I am addicted—
in your shadow
are those
peaceful, easy
feelings

I love your body—
all of it—
and I love
what it does
to mine

Joy

so engulfed am I
in your love
that I ride high
on the waves of freedom

my heart knows
ever crescending
joy like majestic,
cresting breakers
    and
the albatross
of fear
has flown,
leaving the
waters
of my soul
to the
gentle sandpiper

         . . . .

my life is altered
by the touch
of your hand,
as are the
silent,
shifting
sands
sculptured
by the touch
of the wind

from and out
of you
has my love
grown
until like the
amoeba
it is an entity
of its own

. . . .

and if tears
from my mind
should fall
they will be like
diamonds of sunlight
sparkling
on the green sea

with no beginning
and no ending
the sea creates
an infinite
golden horizon—

so
very trifling
compared to
my love
for you

In my
wildest imagination,

it could not
have been
better

P.S. I love you

*Sometimes,
Love Just Creates~*

Little Boys & Big Dogs

never there was
a little boy
or a big dog
that could overlook
a puddle of water—
both seem to find
in the mighty
depths
of that puddle
a world
to create—
and to conquer—
a world
in which to romp
like there was
nothing
beyond now
and now
    and now
        and now ...

The Lure of the Dunes

silent, shifting sands
sculptured by sea breezes
silent — almost
the sands breathe and whisper
their awesome beauty
to all who love and
will listen

tall grasses wave
softly, so softly,
framing the magnificent face
of the dunes
shapes, shadows,
soft curving mounds
like a lovers body

. . . .

gleaming white grains,
warmed by day
from the sun,
stretch forever
and don a cloak
of orange and gold
and pink at dusk

and at night
enfolded and released
by the sensuous arms
of the ocean fog,
the Dunes lie
mystically silver under a
gauze of moonlight

court the Dunes
only if lasting love
is truly what you seek
and if your spirit
is free to fly—
once touched,
you will forever return

My Friend

I thought
about you today
you floated softly
into my mind
and gently caressed
my memory
it was pleasant—
I asked you to stay

rough and raw
like a cowboy hero
you always walked
tall as a mountain
strong and proud
with aristocratic grace,
just spittin' energy
all over the place

. . . .

like good Drambuie
on a winter night,
your special gift
was your warmth
always there
for anyone in need —
not too much
and never too little

perhaps I remember
most of all
your smile —
not the one on your lips,
but the one that
twinkled in your eyes —
it reflected your mind
that I loved to touch

Another Love~

A Masterpiece

of our creations, each of us
    is rightly proud
they are gifts to the world
    the world can laud
my gifts are varied and many
    (not all fabulous!)—
paintings to warm, words to explore—
    gourmet food a plus
one creation is very special,
    perhaps beyond all other—

'twas the day to a "dried up bird"
    I became a mother
nearly eighteen years later
    a swan is definitely what you are,
the finished product more than
    just mine by far
so exquisitely rare is the
    beauty you possess,
even words of prose are not
    adequate to express

you are the "gentle" in the
    touch of a butterfly—
you are the "harmony" in
    the strains of music—
and "strength" in the arms
    of the tallest oak tree.

. . . .

(you are "moody and bitchy"
    sometimes, of course,
but flaws in creations are
    the character strokes!)
you are the "imagination"
    in the mind of man—
you are the "mushrooms" on
    top of the steak—

I am grateful for the sanity
    you give to my space
and thankful for each (almost)
    day I see your face
when one day you fly to a
    "creating place" of your own,
take with you my respect and
    love earned by you alone.
but don't expect to fly totally
    from our association,
after all, an investment have I
    in my very special creation.

Acknowledgement and Dedication

It's funny how we know, or rather don't know, the people closest to us. Or even, how we protect ourselves and don't let people really know us ... maybe only a chosen few, if they're lucky. I think that is part of the "illusion."

Mom's first child, I was 17 when my youngest brother was born. There were four more in between. The world changed tremendously and a lot of "life" happened during the time that spanned my birth and his. And then a lot more "life" happened while I was growing into an adult with my own family and Mom was still working on raising hers. She was going her way, I was going mine.

My "illusion" of Mom was that she was a very serious parent who didn't cut any slack. She had the highest standards imaginable and I felt I could never reach them. She was the most talented and capable person I knew and I guess, maybe, as a result, my own judgments didn't cut her much slack either ... maybe I didn't cut myself much slack.

I have always loved her and respected her tremendously, but never "knew" her until recently. We have been put together at this point in "life" in a special way for which I am so very grateful; an opportunity for us to know each other as mother and daughter, friends and even professionals. There is no room for the illusions now.

I found Mom's beautifully handwritten book of poetry shortly after I moved here to be with her. Imagine how my breath was taken away at my first reading!? Here were all the "insides" of Mom that we kids didn't get a peek at. Of course I knew she had feelings, after all we both cry at sappy movies. But here was Mom in all her vulnerability and honest beauty.

Aside from her beautiful handwriting, I knew these poems to be hers right away because I know of many of those things she talks about; the people, the places and the situations. It was also a picture of my own life. Certainly different people, places and situations, but my, how we were suddenly alike!

I held her book closely for two months trying to decide what to do with this treasure. Finally, with her permission and a little input, I published it to share with the world and, mostly, my sister and brothers.

I hope those that read this beautiful book will share a little passion and a different view of all people surrounding them. I hope Moms book can help the world learn to consider both the "illusions" and the "insides."

I hope my sister and brothers treasure this book as Moms heart. Life is hard and we are formed from both good and bad experiences. In the end all we have is love, if we are lucky, and if that is what we choose. The rest doesn't really matter. Let this passion be what you hold now and keep after she is gone from this world. Let it be what we pass on to our own families. Let this be Moms legacy to us and the world.

I love you, Mom.

Kim

978-0-595-47719-7
0-595-47719-4

Made in the USA
Lexington, KY
02 December 2013